Creating a Vision for Your School

Moving from Purpose to Practice

A Lucky Duck Book

Creating a Vision
for Your School

Sarah Bainbridge

P·C·P
Paul Chapman
Publishing

Paul Chapman Publishing
A SAGE Publications Company
1 Oliver's Yard
55 City Road
London EC1Y 1SP

SAGE Publications Inc.
2455 Teller Road
Thousand Oaks, California 91320

SAGE Publications India Pvt Ltd.
B-42, Panchsheel Enclave
Post Box 4109
New Delhi 110 017

Commissioning Editor: Barbara Maines

Editorial Team: Barbara Maines, Sarah Lynch

Designer: Jess Wright

A catalogue record for this book is available from the British Library

Library of Congress Control Number 2006936943

ISBN 978 1 4129 2019 3

ISBN 978 1 4129 2020 9 (pbk)

Printed on paper from sustainable resources

Printed in Great Britain by The Cromwell Press Ltd, Trowbridge, Wiltshire

8/10/11

Contents

Foreword

It gives me great pleasure, as Head teacher at Air Balloon Hill Junior School, to write the foreword for this book written by my Deputy, Sarah Bainbridge.

Our school has traditionally enjoyed a high level of pupil achievement and it was far from clear at the outset how further work on our vision could benefit us. However, having seen the results of all the hard work that Sarah and the staff have put into this project I can now safely say that we need not have worried! Having a vision seems to act as a lubricant to everything we do, from the quality of the teaching right down to the cleanliness of the playground. We now all share a common view point on the direction our school should take and the final destination on which we should all focus. It is important that everyone shares this strategic viewpoint (not just the management team) and the methods outlined in this book show how this has been achieved. Through careful consultation with staff, students, parents, carers and governors, and the subsequent implementation of many good ideas, our school has benefited since this work was started. I therefore recommend this book as a source of inspirational ideas and practical actions that you too can take to make your school a better place.

Brian Phillips, Head teacher, Air Balloon Hill Junior School, Bristol

1. Introduction

About this book

Why write a book about creating a meaningful vision and positive ethos within a school? I think the first reason lies in the beneficial results that such an exercise can have within a school.

Having spent over 25 years within the teaching profession and having taught in a variety of primary schools I have observed that success is born from positive ethos. This ethos is generated by a shared and agreed vision between stakeholders combined with shared accountability and a sense that everyone feels valued.

My professional studies during my teaching career reaffirmed these observations. Part of my BA (Hons) degree focused upon the need to foster positive relationships and it was during this period that I felt fortunate to be tutored in Teacher Effectiveness and Behaviour Management by Barbara Maines and George Robinson. The practical application of their methods and techniques have been invaluable during my teaching career and have since proved equally useful to the whole process of creating and implementing a vision.

It was whilst studying for my NPQH qualification that I became aware that it is the shared vision and values of a school that shape and support the whole decision making process within it. In 2002 I was fortunate to become Deputy Head at Air Balloon Hill Junior School in Bristol and it was here that I had the opportunity to put into practice all that I had learnt previously. Below is an extract from a recent Ofsted report which gives a picture of the type of school Air Balloon is.

Description of Air Balloon Hill – Ofsted 2002

This is a larger than average junior school catering for 332 pupils aged between seven and eleven. There are only ten more girls than boys but there is a marked imbalance in the number of boys and girls in some year groups. Pupils are organised into 12 classes each with a single age group. The eleven-year olds are taught mathematics in sets, teaching groups organised according to how much pupils already understand about the subject. The majority of pupils is white, some are of mixed ethnicity and eleven pupils are Black British. All pupils are fluent English speakers. Fourteen per cent of pupils are eligible for free school meals; this is broadly average. About 17 per cent of pupils (broadly average) are on the special educational needs register; about eight per cent have significant learning difficulties and two per cent have a statement of special educational needs. The main difficulties include moderate learning difficulties, emotional and communication difficulties and some specific learning problems. The school serves a stable community and there is very little movement of pupils other than at the usual times.

At an early stage it was decided to make use of local educational consultants to assist us in our journey and, as I had previous experience of her methods, the logical choice for me was Barbara Maines. Thanks to Barbara and her 'wise words' (and of course the support of everyone at the school) the whole process proved to be successful and is continuing to be so.

It was from all these positive experiences that I was prompted to record the journey that we undertook as a school so that others may benefit from our experiences. The main purpose of this book therefore is to outline how one school approached the problem of creating a vision together with lessons learned and advice to others who may be considering a similar venture. My second reason for writing this book is related to my belief in the universal applicability of the approach we adopted. As I embarked upon this task I soon became aware that a flexible, easy to manage approach could be of use in a variety of environments and not limited just to schools. I feel sure that, with a small shift in emphasis, the tools and techniques we used could easily be applied to any organisation.

How should you use this book? Well this depends largely on your current position within the process. The book provides a step-by-step account of events as they occurred. For those who are considering a similar venture from scratch it should be an easy matter to simply follow what we did and draw ideas and lessons learned from it. The book also contains templates for all the important documents we used which could be used to 'kick-start' a new initiative.

Those who have some experience of this process, or who are part way through it, could simply refer to the completed examples from each of our sessions for a source of ideas. The book also outlines a 'road map' for success, a typical guided recall exercise and a ten point checklist of essential things to remember. I think these will be useful to anyone involved in a similar venture, regardless of where they are in the process.

Of course, many of the techniques and ideas discussed can be used on their own and applied to an on-going situation – not just in schools.

We certainly learnt a great deal from the experience and in the process also had a lot of fun. I hope you do too!

What is a vision?

Someone once said that, 'Vision is seeing the masterpiece while you are mixing the paints.' It is the process of taking in the current big picture and trying to envision a different future state. Because it is essentially concerned with forward thinking it should become part of the normal strategic planning process for any school. If done correctly, it will draw upon the beliefs, goals and environment of the school and should form the backbone of a positive and inspiring system.

In terms of a school a vision may be defined as:

- an optimistic yet realistic dream of what we would like our school to be

- a preferred future state

- a stated goal that provides direction.

As organisations in industry have been using vision and mission for a long time now it might be useful to examine a typical example of a vision statement drawn from this sector.

> The Ford Motor Company's vision is: ...'to become the world's leading consumer company for automotive products and services.'

A typical example of vision statements drawn from education however might be as follows.

> 'We aim to inspire a thirst for learning, the confidence to achieve and to build a caring community,' or, 'Learning and living together in a happy, caring and stimulating environment.'

The important thing to remember is that each statement is specific to the organisation or school and should mean something special to them. With most organisations trying to be the best in their field this is sometimes difficult to do but is nevertheless a worthwhile aim.

Benefits to be gained from 'visioning'

'Vision without action is a daydream. Action without vision is a nightmare.'
Japanese proverb

Although the process and outcomes of creating a vision may seem vague and superfluous, the longer-term benefits are significant and very real. In particular creating a vision helps a school to break free of convention and encourages thinking 'outside the box'. In order to do this you will need to undertake the process of 'visioning' (as it is sometimes called) in a safe and secure environment where new ideas are encouraged and possibly innovative ways of working are explored.

Visioning also supports long-term strategic planning, largely by avoiding the common stop-start approach to school development that can be so disruptive and counter-productive. Visioning on the other hand, by its very nature is not a short-term, knee-jerk reaction to imposed change (possibly for the worse) but rather a catalyst for carefully planned change (hopefully for the better).

Another important outcome from successful visioning is that it helps define the schools direction and inherent purpose. It alerts everyone in the school to their 'reason for being' and makes it clear where their efforts should be directed. Stakeholders in particular are considered vital to successful visioning and, of course, without them most plans or initiatives would never be successfully realised. As we shall see, the full involvement of stakeholders is essential for a successful outcome.

As visioning should involve everyone then it should also encourage a widespread interest and commitment. Typically people should feel they not only have a stake in the school's success but that they also 'own' the outcomes from visioning. This, of course, assists in building confidence in the future of the school and promotes a sense of loyalty and pride.

The bottom line should be an improvement in efficiency and productivity within the school – something everyone will agree is a good idea!

In summary the main benefits of creating a vision statement are to:

- unify people at all levels toward a shared goal
- bring focus and clarity to our desired future
- energise teams to achieve a common purpose
- develop communications and a common set of values throughout the school

Drawbacks and cautionary notes

As with all processes there are risks that, if not identified and resolved, can seriously devalue the process and the eventual outcomes. This book will document the issues we faced and the way in which we overcame them but for the record it might be useful to highlight some common 'vision killers' here.

One common vision killer is a slavish adherence to tradition. The past is safe but the future is full of doubt and fear – so why not just do what we've always done? History tells us a great deal but we need to progress and move on. Although we should always be aware of lessons from the past, we must also bear in mind that 'yesterday's solutions won't be good enough for tomorrow's problems'!

Fear of ridicule can also be a major obstacle to the visioning process. However, if visioning is conducted in a safe and creative environment then fear of looking foolish should evaporate as people become more confident to put forward new ideas without ridicule. Initially, an attitude that 'no idea is too ridiculous or crazy' is a healthy one to adopt if you truly want to seek something new. Later you may decide as a group to reject or postpone the least desirable ideas without fear of sapping people's self-confidence but ridicule encountered early on in visioning will lead to poor results.

You may also encounter so-called 'naysayers' who habitually seem to offer a negative and possibly even aggressive attitude to anything new. These individuals need careful handling as, once again, they can create havoc with the whole process. One particularly useful technique is to identify their specific area of competence and make good use of it. This supports the concept of ownership and you will find that busy people tend not to have much time to moan!

Outlined below is a real-life example of how a lack of momentum can also cause slow progress or even a total lack of progress towards your goals.

Rejoining class after breaktimes

Lining children up in the playground before entering the building had always been done and had always caused anxiety for all concerned:

the Head teacher as he had to stand guard over the whole school whilst staff assembled, the staff as they had to calm jostling children in their lines and the children as they were pushed and shoved and coped with the ensuing scuffles.

The obvious answer was to jettison the whole idea of lining up and find a more relaxed method of entering the school.

The decision was made for staff to collect their classes informally by going into the playground and holding a hand high. The children were then able to follow their teacher into the school in a friendly relaxed manner avoiding previous rowdy entrances of the past.

At the start this idea worked really well. However, in a short space of weeks this system began to collapse as some children were failing to wait for their teacher before entering the school, resulting in 'traffic jams' outside classroom doors.

It was at this point a more established member of staff voiced the opinion that this 'new system' was not working and that we should go back to the old method of collection.

It was clear that change was uncomfortable for this teacher who was reluctant to analyse the reasons why this new system was failing.

Fortunately, the Head teacher could see its benefits and was ready to look for practical solutions to the problem. After some discussion it became clear where the problem lay.

Staff were not collecting their classes at the same time so some children became anxious when they saw other children entering the school before them and thought that they had missed their teacher. This resulted in children entering the school without their teacher.

It was decided that at the correct time for entry into school the Head teacher would go to the staff room and ensure all staff left together. The Deputy remained in the playground to ensure children waited for their teacher.

After a while the routine became established and everything began to work more smoothly with fewer problems when entering the school.

Naturally this innovation would need monitoring and tweaking where and when necessary.

Without doubt this change was a change for the better that may have been blocked by fear of the new.

It is always tempting to return to the 'known' as it is safer to fail in a way that is understood. Sufficient time therefore needs to be taken to allow innovation to work coupled with a willingness to adapt and persevere when necessary.

Another block to realising the vision can be staff apathy. As we all know, in the teaching profession this can be born of sheer fatigue! Increasingly staff are under pressure to achieve more and more in their time at the workplace and may feel they are too burdened by routine day-to-day tasks to worry about a vision. It is easy to feel that there is not enough time or energy to enable the vision. This should not be allowed to occur. Time and, if necessary, money must be set aside in order to achieve success.

The real-life example below shows how a lack of funds, for example, can completely halt progress.

Case study

Two members of staff volunteered to see that plants were put in and around the school building. This was added to our list of short-term targets. When we came to review the progress made on our targets it was found that no progress had been made.

The two people responsible said that they were unable to achieve their target as they had not been provided with enough resources. When asked what they needed they said money to buy the plants and time out of class to buy and organise them. The financial issue could be solved easily enough with money being made available for the task. However, the time out of class was a trickier issue. With PPA time already in place and time out of class for staff development, this was going to be an added drain on the school's resources. Not only would the school have to pay for extra supply cover but also the children would be losing their teacher at an important time with SATs around the corner.

It is vital that each step towards the vision is seen to be achievable within the constraints of the working day. Careful planning and assignment of responsibilities to those with an interest in the task all help to achieve this but ultimately visioning must be given the priority it deserves to succeed. Initially it will require commitment of extra time but if successful could well help to reduce the routine workload and make life easier. This is similar to the person who is too busy to attend a course on time management hence denying themselves a possible avenue of escape.

It is also common to find that organisations employ VINO – Vision In Name Only! Everyone has heard of this thing called a vision but no one knows what it is or why it's important. Visioning is then treated as a paper exercise, as another job we have to do to keep the authorities happy and, once done, something we can safely ignore. This is unfortunate as the time and effort required to create a vision is then wasted. Why not spend just a little more time and effort making sure it is embedded and doing something useful?

I think it is also important to bear in mind that you will need to develop and apply a range of supportive techniques in order to achieve success. Some of these are clearly associated with the visioning process (e.g. guided recall) whilst others are not obviously so (e.g. the 'self-concept' approach). As long as the method works for you this doesn't matter – just use it.

Finally, as mentioned earlier, visioning is allied to strategic thinking so one aspect that must be guarded against at all costs is negative, short-term thinking. If your visioning is to work at all then a long-term strategic approach needs to be engendered. How this is achieved is something akin to baking a cake (not easy) but hopefully the rest of the book will show ways in which it can be done!

Conclusions

- A vision can be defined as a preferred future state that everyone agrees with and works towards.

- Visioning is not just a paper exercise – action is needed for it to work.

- Visioning must lead to positive change if it is to be beneficial and worthwhile.

- If carried out successfully, visioning supports the strategic direction of the school.

2. What We Did

Historical events that led to this project – what was learnt?

Air Balloon Hill had previously considered its vision and ethos. However, it was felt that this early work needed to be reviewed. With the arrival of a number of new staff (including me) there was a need to review progress, secure commitment and hence define the school's ultimate direction.

From the start it was clear to me that the school was successful and benefited from strong leadership, as the extract from Ofsted, below, clearly shows.

> This continues to be a good school... it is well led and managed… there is a strong shared determination to sustain current rate of improvement (Ofsted 2002).

However, we were made aware of the need to re-examine and clarify our vision when our School Improvement Officer asked if all our stakeholders were aware of it. We were doubtful as we ourselves were unsure of exactly what the current vision was.

Borne of this uneasy situation we decided to engage in a new programme of vision and ethos training.

Initial staff reaction varied greatly but was mainly one of cynicism ('We've done it before,') and disbelief ('What's that?').

> 'I felt it was going to be merely a paper exercise with nothing useful at the end of it,' Teacher Yr3
>
> 'I didn't want just meaningless words in a vision statement,' Teacher Yr 6

This did not surprise me as vision and ethos sessions in my previous schools appeared to merely be 'going through the motions' without transferring values into actions.

For example:

> ### Case study (from a previous school)
>
> During one inset session it was decided that the wearing of school uniform should be enforced to enhance the image of the school. Although this was minuted it was never acted upon. Even though the decision was unanimous it simply did not work. Why? Well largely because the parents and the children had not taken part in the consultation process. Those needed to make it work were not involved.

Faced with this somewhat negative view of vision and ethos training I knew that the programme that I planned to deliver needed to be relevant and 'hands on'. Staff had to feel that their thoughts and opinions had been heard and included. Also they had to be able to see the benefits of each session immediately. They needed to see that their ideas were making a real practical difference to the school both inside and outside the classroom. Finally, they must feel part of the shared dream for the school.

Road map

Overview of events as they occurred

The events as they occurred are summarised in the table below. Of course, the sequence of events and the methods we used do not need to be copied exactly in order to achieve success. They are merely offered here as a guide and can be modified to suit the situation as needed.

Phase	Event	Purpose
Preparation	Inset Day 1 **Setting the Scene**	To remind ourselves of our purpose as a school. To understand the reasons for creating a vision. To generate enthusiasm and to agree the need to make things better. To ensure that any vision is shared with the children and based on our relationships with them. This initial session was facilitated by consultant experts.
Preparation	Staff Inset Session **Generating Ideas from Staff**	To identify what needs to be changed by using a 'guided recall' exercise, (comparing where we are to where we want to be).
Preparation	**Generating Ideas from Other Stakeholders**	To gain ideas from pupils, governors, admin and support staff and to ensure they had a sense of 'ownership'.
Preparation	**Consultation with Parents**	To ensure that parents were included and able to make a contribution. To ensure that parents had a sense of 'ownership'.
Preparation	Staff Inset Session **Identifying Common Values**	To categorise our agreed values into the four main areas that are essential for the successful functioning of a school To develop Values Statements in the 4 key areas from above that reflect our agreed values

Phase	Event	Purpose
Planning	Staff Inset Session **Generation of Value Statements and Initial Vision Statement**	To clarify in writing the core underpinning values and to prioritise subsequent actions. To generate in initial vision statement which everyone shared and could be developed further.
Planning	Inset Day 2 **Barriers to Progress**	To identify factors that may inhibit or prevent desired change. To enhance listening and problem solving skills.
Planning	Staff Inset Session **Areas for Action**	To sort and select actions and put them under our four values headings: • Environment • Relationships • Teaching and Learning • Aesthetic and Spiritual
Action	Staff Inset Session **Prioritising and Allocating Responsibilities**	To prioritise actions and who will take responsibility and action them.
Assess and Review	Staff Inset Session **Review of Progress**	To take stock of achievements to date. To report on those targets achieved, those in-hand and those which have yet to start.
Assess and Review	Staff Inset Session **Assessment of Benefits**	To assess what has been gained and what still needs to be done.
Assess and Review	**Where Next?**	To look back and decide what went well and what we could have done better. To plan for the next phase, including the setting of new targets. To publish and advertise our achievements to all stakeholders and the outside community.

3. Setting the Scene
– Inset Day 1

Introduction

In order to promote enthusiasm, and set the scene, it was felt that we needed to bring in an external expert to facilitate this introductory inset session. We felt an external consultant would allow us to think 'outside the box' and not get bogged down by parochial issues.

Barbara Maines was chosen for this role. Why? She not only had vast experience as a successful Educational Psychologist but she also had first hand knowledge of our school, (having skilfully managed several of our most disaffected pupils in the past). She was also highly respected for her contributions in the educational field, not only as a lecturer but also as an established author.

One might normally expect this initial session to be all about ideas generation. Although this certainly happened it was actually more about exploring our initial reasons for working on a shared vision. Our starting point would then be established and our reasons for embarking on this journey would be clear.

Aims of session

- To remind ourselves of our purpose as a school.
- To understand the reasons for creating a vision.
- To generate enthusiasm and to agree the need to make things better.
- To ensure that any vision is shared with the children and based on our relationships with them.

What we did

This initial session involved all teaching staff and focused mainly on our 'customers' (i.e. the pupils) and the importance of the children's 'self-concept', in other words how they felt about themselves and their sense of value within the community. The success of our vision and ethos training was felt to hinge on these key stakeholders being able to trust each other and respect all points of view.

As an exercise we initially looked at past incidents that had turned us against certain aspects of our own education. We quickly realised that a negative interaction can easily lead to a damaged self-image as the example below illustrates.

> ### Activity: Childhood Memories
>
> One of the activities we undertook included remembering a time when we were pupils and had been made to feel bad about ourselves, often due to careless words or the actions of unwitting teachers. This activity was very revealing as it quickly became apparent that we had all suffered in this way as children, even to the extent of remembering names and the actual words spoken. This frightening discovery made it apparent how easy it is for we as adults to cause lasting damage to a child's self-concept just through a simple dismissive comment or thoughtless action.

We then shared experiences of how pupil behaviour could be improved through the promotion of a positive self-concept and how we could maintain relationships through the use of 'I' messages. In my experience 'I' messages are a highly successful way of communicating, both in a constructive and reassuring way. The message itself may just be that of 'confirmation' but would nevertheless also contain an expression of one's feelings.

For example:

'I feel very proud when you write so neatly and carefully.'

In this case the message becomes personal and, in the process, potentially precious.

> Positive 'I' messages are not just for pupils and by expressing your true feelings the messages you send are more likely to be effective in any relationship. There is no trick or special skill… just start with an 'I' and say how you feel. (Maines & Robinson)

I have also found 'I' messages to be extremely useful in situations when unacceptable behaviour needs to be addressed. These messages need to delivered in three parts - behaviour, effect and feelings.

For example:

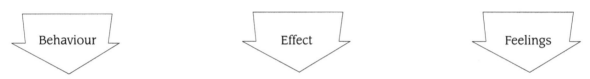

'When you play with your ruler.............. I am unable to concentrate ....and this makes me feel irritable.'

Here the situation is confronted openly by an expression of how one feels. The response may not be what is required (e.g. so what?). However, it is more likely to be positive as there little opportunity for confrontation and a clear understanding of the negative impact of the actions.

> **'I' messages can:**
>
> Communicate feelings
>
> Reduce likelihood of confrontation
>
> Opens up possibility of discussion
>
> Protect the self concept of the pupil
>
> Allow the adult to stay calm and express feelings.
>
> (Maines & Robinson)

Case Study – the self-concept

A pupil entered my Year 6 class in September. He had already gained the label 'trouble maker'. This worried me as I believe that all children have a need to succeed and be approved of and that this child was simply performing against the 'norm'. Once in class he certainly proved to be infuriatingly slow at organising himself and when hurried would display challenging behaviour. It was easy to see how he could become every teacher's nightmare.

It was at the end of the Christmas term that the true nature of the problem became evident. When asked to organise Christmas cards into class groups, a simple sorting job, he was just unable to achieve the task. When I asked him what the problem was he replied that he was hopeless at organising things and as a result he had just panicked.

Here at last was the key to his negative behaviour. Unable to organise himself, he had been judged as being uncooperative and this had then generated a whole series of negative behaviours. Compounding this problem he was the fact that he was also very tired having many late nights unable to sleep. When asked why, it was evident that he was worrying and feeling unable to control his life.

His self-concept was at rock bottom with little or no belief in himself. This situation needed to be tackled urgently as secondary school was looming ever closer. My task was to help him to believe in himself again as I believed he was an intrinsically able child. I set into motion a plan of action.

I sat him close to me so I could prepare him for a class instruction before I spoke to the main class. This meant he would have his pen or pencil ready at the same time if not before everyone else – an opportunity for praise!

Being close to me gave me the opportunity for a reassuring smile or a wink of approval without compromising his 'street cred'. This often prompted a smile in reply. This positive relationship had to be continually reinforced. When things went wrong, as they were bound to at times, it was vital he could accept my disapproval of his behaviour without feeling a loss of my approval of him as a person. The use of 'I' statements proved to be invaluable during these times. Both parties were able to express their thoughts and feelings without jeopardising this important bond.

His work quickly improved and he found that he no longer needed to act out inappropriate behaviour to gain peer group approval and he was now regarded as a class leader due to ability. Having universal respect and positive attention proved to be a more satisfying reward.

Support from other stakeholders also helped to make this difference. His mother was made aware of his difficulties and was supportive of the school's actions. She tried to ensure that he had early nights to bed with a book. This was a great help.

The school SENCo was also involved with offering small group/one to one support in order to boost self-image and prepare for KS3.

A Learning Mentor from the local secondary school was also able to offer him preparation sessions for KS3.

Feeling that he now had a value made a huge difference to his school life. Not only did he make positive contributions in class lessons but also during school council discussions. In his own way he now felt able to give of himself and so help the us as a community to reach its ultimate goals.

This case study highlights not only the need to communicate effectively but also the importance of empathising and listening.

An interesting follow-up activity involved us sitting next to a colleague with whom we had minimal contact with during our working day. The task was to find three things that we had in common, the more unusual the better! After ten minutes in our pairs, and with lots of chatter and laughter, we all succeeded at the task. Suddenly colleagues were discovering that they didn't just have school in common but maybe a favourite flavour pizza or same colour of bathing costume! How little we truly knew about each other.

The consequence of this exercise was twofold. Not only were we suddenly aware that we had more in common than we thought, (helping to draw us closer as a team), but also it highlighted how little opportunity is taken to talk and listen to each other whilst at work

The question that then came to mind was 'what about the rest of the stakeholders?' How well do we in fact know our own pupils, parents or other stakeholders? If we were embarking on a journey towards a shared vision we needed to ensure we were truly communicating to everyone. This realisation led to a number of subsequent sessions being devoted to involving the stakeholders.

Self-concept approach and the Hierarchy of Needs

It may be useful at this stage to see how the self-concept approach supports children's development by considering a well-known theory of motivation – that of Abraham Maslow.

Maslow proposed his so-called 'hierarchy of needs' after studying the behaviour of monkeys, (see diagram below). He was particularly interested in motivational factors and formed a pyramid of needs with which to illustrate his theory, (see below). He proposed that the lower-level needs must be satisfied before the higher levels can act as motivators. Once the lower levels have been satisfied then they no longer act as motivators and people start to look for higher level motivators.

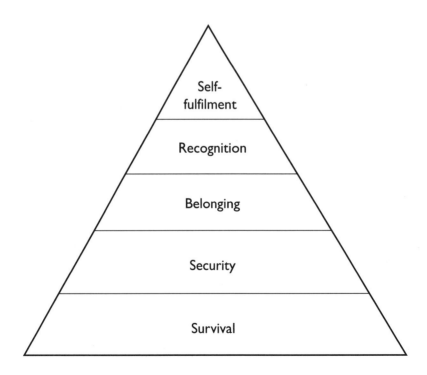

The school is obliged to satisfy the most basic level of survival needs – e.g. those of food, water and shelter. Indeed, not much can be achieved if these needs are not met! A similar situation exists when we move up to the next level of need – that of security. Once again, it is every school's duty to provide for these needs. However, if a child is being bullied, for example, then the need for security cannot be met until the situation is resolved. This is definitely an area where a practical application of the self-concept approach can help.

This brings us to the next two levels of need where the self-concept can also be very effective – that of belonging and recognition. It is here that we can support the child's development so that they are able to start moving towards the top and final level – self-fulfilment. Once at this level the child can finally begin to reach her full potential thanks, once again, to the supportive role of the self-concept approach lower down. So the self-concept approach can be used at just about any level and ultimately supports the ultimate goal – fulfilled children.

But the story does not stop there. Many people have suggested that the pyramid of needs is not closed at the top but open, indicating that there is in fact no limit to what can be ultimately achieved. Food for thought!

Conclusions

The main aim of the session (to generate interest and enthusiasm) had been met and staff were now looking forward to the next session.

The activities undertaken during this day ensured that we became aware of the need to understand a problem before we can start to fix it. To do this we need to listen and work with others.

The ability to use listening skills and to problem solve needed to be developed in order to ensure that everyone was included in the quest for our shared vsion and values. This was planned to be covered in the next visit from Barbara and her colleague George Robinson.

It was clear from this first inset session that staff had gained the enthusiasm to make changes that would allow all stakeholders to feel valued and included. All of a sudden there was an active drive towards the creation of positive relationships throughout the school. Everyone went away busily practising 'I' statements and fed back to me their success over the following weeks.

In summary then the lessons learnt from this session were as follows:

- Consider running a preliminary session which aims to 'set the scene'.
- For best results keep the session short and focused but also fun and relaxed.
- Use exercises that explore new perspectives and ideas.
- Use an external facilitator wherever possible.
- Be prepared to be surprised!

4. Generating Ideas from Staff
– Staff Inset Session

Introduction

Now was the time to establish what sort of school we wanted Air Balloon Hill Junior to be. Did we all want similar things for our school or were we each looking for a different end state?

This question could only be answered by understanding what we as stakeholders considered to be the ultimate desirable qualities of a school environment. We needed to extract our common values in an atmosphere of safety and inclusion.

Aim of session

- To identify what could be changed and to compare where we were currently to where we would like to be.

What we did

To achieve the above aim I devised a virtual tour/guided recall exercise. The text for this is included at the end of this chapter.

The staff were encouraged to sit comfortably and close their eyes (if they wished). They were told that they were going to take a tour around a perfect school. At certain points of the tour there would be a pause, a time to think and mentally note their thoughts and feelings.

I then read the virtual tour text slowly and clearly and without any emotional cues. The text described the journey around an imaginary school. The visit started by entering at the main gate and then crossing the playground to the main door. Once within the building the listener was then taken around the school interior, including classrooms and hall. This virtual visit was completed as the listener was taken back outside, at the end of the school day, and leaving finally through the front gate again.

Short rests punctuated this journey (highlighted words on the given example). These were vital as they allowed a breathing space for thoughts and feelings to emerge.

Afterwards, the staff were asked to discuss their thoughts and feelings in pairs and record the most significant of these on 'sticky' notes. These were then placed into a simple framework which related directly to the areas covered within the recall exercise (see next section). For example, any strong feelings gained when walking across the playground were placed within that corresponding section and so on until all ideas had been classified.

The key rule at this stage was that all ideas were valid and that none were to be discarded as impractical.

Frame for sticky notes

The table overleaf shows the frame used to classify the ideas generated above. This was ideally suited to our particular school environment but could easily be adapted to suit your own needs.

Hall - should be:	Playground – should be:
Classrooms – should be:	Inside the building – should be:

This frame was drawn out on a large piece of paper and then stuck to the wall. This allowed all staff to attach their sticky-notes at the same time. This proved to be a fun way to share each others ideas. I chose this method rather than using the interactive white board as it felt more 'hands on', ensuring that there was plenty of movement and practical activity for the staff. This helped to maintain interest and keep up the momentum – essential for success.

Conclusion

The very nature of this exercise allowed for the free exchange of thoughts and ideas. Everyone had the opportunity to contribute to the session with some staff highly enthused by the chance to share their thoughts with others.

'I felt the session easy to follow, I was inspired. I actually came out and felt my voice was heard.' – teacher Y3

By the end of this session our aim had been achieved. A large number of excellent ideas for our school had come to the fore and the school we wanted had been revealed through moments of quiet reflection and the sharing of ideas via a secure and enjoyable path.

NB. In order to avoid unnecessary repetition, the results from this session, (and those from other stakeholders) can be seen in Chapter 5 – Generating Ideas from Other Stakeholders.

Virtual tour/guided recall – walkthrough

The text shown in the next section was read out loud during the session. Naturally this is specific to my school's particular circumstances but could easily be adapted for another environment by changing the order of the journey or by altering or adding to the areas visited.

During this exercise it is important to give reflection time for the listeners to appreciate all areas of this 'virtual' world. They really need to 'feel' what they really value in their place of work. Sections highlighted in bold text (yellow on the CD-ROM) indicate where these pauses for reflection and contemplation were inserted.

The open-ended sentence at the conclusion of the recall was deliberately used to draw out personal values that may not have emerged before. Staff created their own endings as they felt appropriate. These short phrases were retained so they could be added to our list of values at a later date.

Virtual tour/guided recall – text

Today we will be visiting our perfect/ideal school. Close your eyes and imagine.

You walk towards the schools main gate – **what do you see? What do you hear? What do you feel?**

Next you push open the gate and walk across the busy playground – **what do you see? What do you hear? What do you feel?**

As you enter the through the main door the whistle blows and the children also enter the school – **what do you see? What do you hear? What do you feel?**

You need to announce your arrival at the office. **How do you get there?**

On the way to the office you pass pupils on their way to their lessons – **what do you see? What do you hear? What do you feel?**

You have now been given permission to spend the day in the school and you set off on a tour of the classrooms (Don't forget a quick stop at the toilet on the way) – **how do you find your way around?**

As you move along the corridors – **what do you see? What do you hear? What do you feel?**

You visit each classroom in turn, as you enter each room – **what do you see? What do you hear? What do you feel?**

You are invited to join the school for assembly – **what do you see? What do you hear? What do you feel?**

After assembly you follow the children outside for play – **what do you see? What do you hear? What do you feel?**

After play you spend some time looking around the outside of the building (Don't forget to say hello the caretaker) – **what do you see? What do you hear? What do you feel?**

You have been invited to lunch in the school dining hall as you sit down – **what do you see? What do you hear? What do you feel?**

Your afternoon is spent on the field where you watch a variety of PE lessons – football, hockey, rounders – you watch the children as they play in their groups – **what do you see? What do you hear? What do you feel?**

As the end of the school day approaches you move back to the playground and stand near the main exit. You can see the whole playground and the cloakrooms from your position. Look carefully as the children leave – **what do you see? What do you hear? What do you feel?**

You follow the children out of the gate. As you leave you promise to return. You realise the school has generated a great sense of well being within you **because…**

5. Generating Ideas from Other Stakeholders

Introduction

The staff were now ready to make changes for the better. However, it was clear from the outset that nothing could change without the full support of other interested parties within the school – e.g. pupils, support and admin staff and of course the Governing Body. This provided the opportunity for staff to use the same virtual tour we used previously within their own classes.

Aim of session

- To gain ideas from other stakeholders in order to support our ideal of universal ownership and commitment within the school.

What we did

Firstly I met with the Governors of the school and took them on the same journey as I had taken the staff during the previous staff inset session. Once the journey was completed the anticipation of action was such that I merely needed to hand over the 'sticky notes' and the discussion of ideas flowed rapidly.

At last the Governors had an opportunity to 'throw caution to the wind' and be creative! This was an extremely exciting moment for me as it was such a pleasure to see lively interest from those people who are often associated with making heavy strategic decisions. The results from this meeting were very useful as the Governors were seeing the school from a different perspective altogether and their ideas were duly added to those of the staff.

The SENCo was pleased to take the support and admin staff through the same journey with similar positive effects. Again, these ideas were added to our ever growing list.

Secondly the staff had the task of taking their classes through the same virtual tour as us. Ideas came thick and fast from all classes. Each teacher managed the details of these class sessions as they felt fit. For example, in some circumstances using sticky-notes was not practical and so staff used an A4 copy of the four main areas for the children to complete in pairs. These were then collated onto one sheet.

A staff meeting was then set aside to allow everyone to share their class responses with staff from parallel year groups (in Air Balloon Hill we have three classes per year). These were finally collated into a single year group response. At the end of this session we shared our year group responses as a whole staff.

At this stage I had a huge collection of responses from all areas of the school. My next job was to sort through all of them. Similar ideas were carefully grouped together. A general consensus about certain aspects of school life became apparent. This allowed me to sift out the core issues for us as a school and from this I drew up a final table that encompassed all these ideas.

I quickly became aware that responses could be divided into practical actions and those which were more of a feeling about what our school should be. The actions section would be needed at a later stage but the feelings and values could be used right away (see next Chapter).

Summary of ideas generated

Hall – should be	Playground and outside –should be
Children sharing performing participation	Laughter and talking
Audience attentive and questioning	Fun
Fresh air	Games
More space	Plants
Quiet	No football
Calm	Wall paintings
Colourful	Quiet shady areas
Relaxing	No litter
Reflective	Happy play
Celebration of life in and outside school	Friendly
Understanding	Smiling
Tolerant	Respectful fair and co-operative
Bright colourful displays of work	Sharing
Cheerful and inviting atmosphere	Stimulating well-kept environment
Class services	Polite language
Light	Care of equipment
Children walking calmly	Football in only one section
Listening and being involved.	Safe and welcoming.

Classrooms – should be	Inside the building – should be
Bright colourful informative interactive displays of children's work	Well kept environment
Well organised, tidy and clean	Scented toilets
Literate environment	Photos of children, achievements and work on display
Busy working atmosphere	Welcoming atmosphere
Happy and productive	Slow quiet calm
Interactive	No pushing –waiting
Enthusiastic - bubbling	Spaces
Unified feeling	Bright colourful
Calm	Green
Friendly	Paper towels
Inspiring	Soft soap - flowery
Positive interaction between all class members including adults	Signs to guide visitors.
Respectful	
Interesting and questioning	
Relaxed	
Smiles and laughter	
Praise	
Quiet and on task.	

Our perfect school should be...

By looking through the final list of responses and also the completion phrases from the end of the virtual tours I drew up a list of values that represented a whole-school consensus on what we wanted our school to be.

This is summarised in the table below:

Calm	Safe
Slow	Quiet
Green	Enthusiastic
Co-operative	Keen to learn
Welcoming	Inspiring
Polite	Hardworking
Considerate	Relaxing
Evolving	Progressive
Understanding	Supportive
Pride in appearance	Cherishing as individuals
Warmth in response	Respectful
Friendly	Interesting
Happy	Excitement in learning
Team Spirit	Confident
Cheerful	Playing together
Fun	Peaceful
Sharing	Exciting
Tidy	Clean
Colourful	Polite

Conclusion

This stage of our vision and ethos journey was truly remarkable and certainly promoted a widespread interest in the process with lots of useful ideas coming forward for later consideration. It was terrific to see everyone fuelled with enthusiasm for change which spurred me on to take the next important step – consultation with the parents.

> 'I enjoyed taking my class on a journey through their perfect school.
> The following discussions were very inspiring and encouraging that we do all want the same for our school.' Teacher Y6

In summary the lessons learnt from this session were as follows:

- No idea is too ridiculous or crazy at this stage.
- Simple exercises (such a virtual tours) should be used to unlock hidden ideas and feelings.
- Involve everyone in the school.
- Classify ideas under main headings such as, classroom, playground, hall, buildings.
- Draw up a list of shared values.

6. Consultation with Parents

Introduction

All the main stakeholders had now been consulted – except for the parents. For those in small schools this could be covered by simply arranging a meeting and then going through the same exercise as all the other stakeholders. Unfortunately this was not possible for us (due to our large size) and I guess this would be the same for many other schools. Due to this fact, and the particular area in which our school is located, it was felt that the parents would be the most difficult group to 'reach'. The majority of our parents work full-time and have very busy lives with little time to give to extra meetings at school or prepare lengthy responses to in-depth questionnaires. Nevertheless they could not be ignored as their commitment was crucial. No change affecting the pupils in a school should be undertaken without parental support as without it your efforts could easily be doomed to failure.

Aims of session

- To ensure that parents were included and able to make a contribution.
- To ensure parents had a sense of 'ownership'.

What we did

I wanted to gain the support and involvement of as many parents as possible. What was needed was a way of gaining ideas without asking them to invest too much time or effort. A letter was designed that fulfilled both these requirements. It comprised of a brief introduction and a diagram of a school surrounded by the values statements we generated earlier.

This proved to be both easy to read and also simple to complete as it only involved circling five values that they felt were important for the school. An opportunity for parents to add their own ideas to our existing list was also considered useful as the parental perspective was such an important one.

Staff handed out copies of this letter to their classes on the same day, explaining the contents and the importance of getting their parents to reply. The pupils were keen for their parents to have a chance to be included in our vision and ethos work and they eagerly took the letters home.

After a week I collected the parental responses. It was a relief to discover that a third of the parents had responded – a very good result! A variety of values were identified by parents and it was interesting to find that by far the most popular values were those that included excitement and inspiration as part of their children's learning.

Conclusion

We had achieved a good overall response from parents. It was clear from the replies received that parents felt the same as the rest of the stakeholders. It was their bias towards a more exciting style of learning within the school that gave us food for thought. It was clear that to fully achieve our aims here we would need to find new ways of involving these important allies.

In summary, the lessons learnt from this session were as follows:

- Don't forget the parents – they are one of the most influential stakeholders.
- You will need to get their ideas with minimal time and effort on their part.
- Don't be surprised by the quality of ideas they generate!

Example of letter to parents

This letter was designed for instant appeal and easy completion. The parents name was needed to ensure there were no 'doubles'. Schools with a wide ethnic mix or having parents with disabilities may need to consider providing this in different formats (translations into other languages or in Braille, for example).

Dear Parents,
As part of our recent vision and ethos training the staff, pupils and governors have been thinking about the values that we would like our school to reflect. We would like to share these with you. Your opinions and ideas are very important to us. Please draw a circle around the five values that you consider most important. Feel free to add to our list if you wish. Please return this form to the office.

Our perfect school should be...

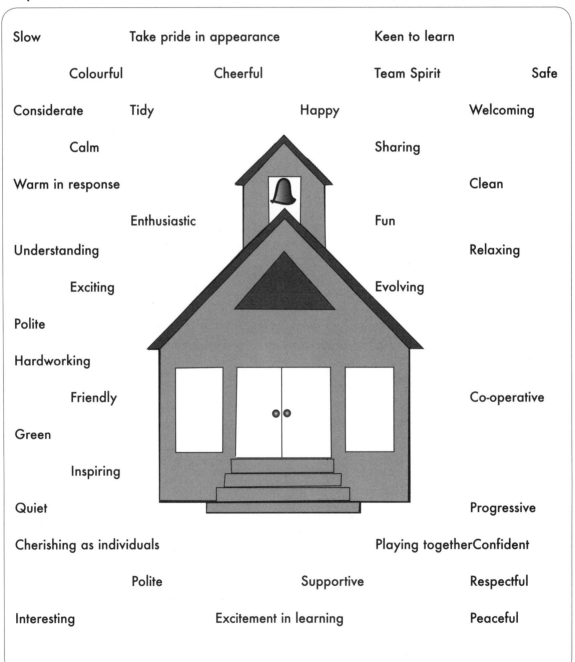

Slow   Take pride in appearance   Keen to learn

Colourful   Cheerful   Team Spirit   Safe

Considerate   Tidy   Happy   Welcoming

Calm   Sharing

Warm in response   Clean

Enthusiastic   Fun

Understanding   Relaxing

Exciting   Evolving

Polite

Hardworking

Friendly   Co-operative

Green

Inspiring

Quiet   Progressive

Cherishing as individuals   Playing togetherConfident

Polite   Supportive   Respectful

Interesting   Excitement in learning   Peaceful

7. Identifying Common Values – Staff Inset Session

Introduction

We had made considerable progress at obtaining views from a wide range of stakeholders. Unfortunately we were unable to include our SMSA's and kitchen staff in our initial sessions as it had been difficult to find the opportunity for consultation. We all recognised that this would need to be rectified in the future.

Nevertheless, using our list of values, we were now ready to form our basic vision statements. It would be from these statements that our overall vision for our school could be formed and which would underpin all future actions.

The four main areas that we felt needed to be considered in a school were:

1. Does it have a 'safe positive environment'?

2. Are 'relationships' positive and productive?

3. Is 'teaching and learning' relevant and of the highest quality?

4. Is there an opportunity for all to experience 'aesthetic and spiritual' aspects of school life?

These four areas were easily identified as important from our list of values. In fact, the categories almost identified themselves! For example, Environment: welcoming, Relationships: respectful, Teaching: progressive, Aesthetic: inspiring.

These headings later became our 'values categories' which were used to identify priorities and assign responsibilities.

Just as a reminder, the values statements which were generated after we decided what 'Our Perfect School Should Be' were as follows.

Calm	Happy	Relaxing
Slow	Team spirit	Progressive
Green	Cheerful	Supportive
Co-operative	Fun	Cherishing as individuals
Welcoming	Sharing	Respectful
Polite	Tidy	Interesting
Considerate	Colourful Safe	Excitement in learning
Evolving	Quiet	Confident
Understanding	Enthusiastic	Playing together
Pride in appearance	Keen to learn	Peaceful
Warmth in response	Inspiring	Exciting
Friendly	Hardworking	Clean
		Polite

Aims of session

- To categorise our agreed values into the four main areas that are essential for the successful functioning of a school.

- To develop summary values statements that reflect our agreed values, under those four areas.

What we did

The staff were divided into three colour coded groups with either green, yellow or blue 'sticky notes'. Each group had to write a value on a 'sticky note' and place it under one of the four main categories outlined above (in a similar way to the previous Guided Recall exercises). This was then repeated for the other values from list.

In order to facilitate this, the frame below was drawn out on a large piece of sugar paper and then stuck to the wall. This allowed all staff to attach their 'sticky-notes' at the same time, which turned out to be a fun way to share each other's ideas.

Safe positive environment	Positive and productive relationships
Teaching and learning	Aesthetic and spiritual

On completion of the task the groups were given ten minutes to look at the other group's choices. If there were any differences of opinion between the group's choices then they had to negotiate or persuade each other to move their values into the other group's category until consensus was reached.

Following this, the groups were asked to decide collectively if any of their values were similar enough to be grouped together. This enabled us to simplify our ideas and focus more clearly on identifying our core values.

We were now ready to compose our vital initial 'Values Statements'.

Each of the three groups of staff were given just one of the above headings to consider and had to complete a leading sentence: 'We want our school to...'

The heading of 'aesthetic and spiritual' was shared by all groups as this was felt to be the least tangible area to tackle and therefore the most difficult to 'sum up'.

The completed sentences were pinned up for all to see and share. After tweaking or adding a few words and phrases we had finally completed the statements that reflected our core values.

These are summarised below.

Safe positive environment

We want Air Balloon Hill Junior School to be a safe, calm, welcoming environment where everyone takes pride in their surroundings.

Positive and productive relationships

We want Air Balloon Hill Junior School to be a happy community with respectful cooperative relationships.

Teaching and learning

We want Air Balloon Hill Junior School to promote excitement in learning through supportive, stimulating teaching that is progressive, constantly evolving.

Aesthetic and spiritual

We want Air Balloon Hill Junior School to be an inspiring environment in which all individuals are cherished.

Birth of a new vision statement

We had agreed on our collective values. The next step was to use these to create our overarching School Vision Statement, by which we could advertise our raison d'etre to the outside world.

By using key words generated in the previous exercises three possible Vision Statements were developed.

> 1. We aim to provide a stimulating learning environment which values and develops all individuals.
>
> 2. We aim to create an exciting learning environment that values and develops everyone.
>
> 3. We aim to provide an inspiring learning environment that values and develops everyone.

After a short discussion it was decided that option 3 was the one that best represented us with the word 'inspiring' being of significant importance to all of us.

Conclusion

The aims of this session were achieved in full and at last we had a Vision Statement. We had ensured that our most important values had been established and organised into a framework that we could easily turn into practical action. Everything that we did within school now should sit beneath at least one of our values statements. From now on our actions needed to reflect our collective principles or we would not be serving the requirements of the stakeholders.

It was also interesting to note that, compared to earlier sessions, we were by this stage all sharing a common goal and beginning to trust each other without fear of ridicule. This led to a consensus being reached much more easily than is normal during collective decision-making meetings.

In summary the lessons learnt from this session were as follows:

- Visioning cannot be rushed – it takes time and effort but is worth it in the end.

- Time and effort spent at the earlier stages pays dividends later on.

- Consensus can and should be reached by this stage.

- Some stakeholders are more difficult to involve than others (perhaps due to their working hours, for example) and should be dealt with in a way which suits them.

- If you fail to involve a group of stakeholders it becomes very difficult to involve them later.

8. Barriers to Progress
– Inset Day 2

Introduction

Whilst we were now ready to decide on the actions we wanted to undertake as a school in order to move towards our new vision we also realised there would be barriers to this. We therefore decided to run this session not only to generate ideas for implementing change but also to address potential barriers.

In all establishments, including schools, there are some routines or organisational procedures that can become a barrier to change. The 'we've always done it this way' mentality had to be challenged. This session, facilitated by external consultants, had come at the right moment as we needed to ensure we were prepared to make some possibly fundamental changes.

As previously discussed within this book, the ability to use listening skills and to problem-solve are vital to the success of projects such as this. We all felt that we would benefit from training in order to develop and enhance our skills in these areas. It was agreed that Barbara Maines and George Robinson were the best people for this job and they were duly invited to run this session.

Aims of session

- To identify factors that may inhibit or prevent desired change.

- To enhance listening and problem-solving skills.

What we did

Blocks to change

The first part of the session involved revisiting our Four Value Statements. The staff were divided into four groups and each group given one of the statements, a large sheet of paper and a marker pen. The task was to consider what present aspects of school life relating to each statement could block desired change. Lively discussion immediately ensued:

- 'How can our environment be safe if your head gets knocked off by a football every time you cross the playground?'

- 'How can teaching and learning be inspiring if we use lots of worksheets?'

- 'How can relationships be respectful if we forget to welcome visitors or open doors for them?'

- 'How can we inspire if we are always in a rush?'

It wasn't long before each of the four large sheets of paper was filled with ideas for achieving the vision statements. These ideas were shared with the whole staff and added to previous ideas for action.

Problem ownership

The next part was run by George who talked about problem ownership. His approach to problem-solving is that you must determine who owns the problem before it can be solved.

As an example he presented a set of problem scenarios and asked us to decide who had ownership of each problem. This proved to be much more tricky than we expected. For interest I include a couple of examples here for you to try.

Who owns the problem, you or the other person?

a)   A student in your class talks and laughs while you are teaching; this irritates you and ruins your concentration.

b)   A student tells you she is bored in your class.

c)   Your head teacher expects you to attend a meeting regardless of previous plans you have made.

Answers:

a) You own the problem as you can't teach effectively in a noisy classroom.

b) The other owns the problem. It is her boredom.

c) You own the problem as you will have to change your plans or incur the displeasure of the head.

If the problem belongs to the other person the technique of 'active listening' would need to be employed. However, if the problem is yours then problem-solving techniques need to be used.

Active listening is a simple concept that involves looking for the real message behind the words and then responding to that hidden message so allowing disclosure of feelings and concerns. For example:

Coded message	Possible real message	Possible answer allowing for safe disclosure
'Did you see how far Carol hit the ball? Well, forget me making the team.'	Discouraged, feels she can't compete.	'So you feel you are not good enough to make the team?' (Maines & Robinson)

Staff were grouped into threes. One person was to disclose a problem (either real or imaginary) the other had to use active listening to explore the problem. The third person acted as observer and had to feed back to the other two on the degree of their success. Everyone had the opportunity to practise active listening and like so many 'simple' concepts it turned out to be very much harder to do than was expected.

Active listening

The next task was set to test how good we were at using this skill of listening when dealing with parents and carers.

Once again we made use of a critical observer to deliver feedback at the end of the activity. One person played the parent and the other the teacher. The parent was given a particular problem, for example, ill health and domestic complications arising from it. The problem was considered to be serious enough to have caused a negative impact on their child's ability to learn.

As far as the teacher was concerned the pupil was underachieving drastically and needed more support from home. It was with some surprise to the teacher that the parent showed little interest in their child's lack of progress, whilst offering lame excuses and simply handing blame back to the teacher. The teacher had to discover the source of the real problem through the use of active listening.

This task was extremely difficult to achieve as the 'parent' was not going to reveal the problem easily. It required careful listening with attention to detail and carefully worded questions in reply. Some found that this process highlighted how as teachers we often view the problem as ours when in reality it belongs to the other person. It emphasised the need to look for the 'real' message when listening to our stakeholders.

Once the problem was identified a problem-solving route would need to be taken. George outlined one possible Six Step Problem-solving Method which if followed should guide the owner towards a successful conclusion. A quick checklist of the main steps involved is shown below.

Six Step Problem-solving Method

1. Defining the problem – understand (using active listening).

2. Generate solutions – brainstorm solutions (however unlikely).

3. Evaluate solutions – select all realistic solutions.

4. Choosing a solution – select best solution.

5. Implement the solution – carry out plan.

6. Assess the success – has it worked?

Conclusion

This session had clearly addressed our need to identify the barriers to progress, to enhance our listening skills and to clarify the problem-solving route. Now we were ready to move the school forward, confident in the knowledge that we had practical techniques to develop and maintain relationships with our stakeholders. We were also now armed with useful strategies to overcome some of the difficulties we might encounter when dealing with these stakeholders.

In summary both the inset days provided by the external consultants had proved to be very useful. Specifically they had taught us how to:

• develop the self-concept of stakeholders, through the use of 'I' messages

• maintain positive communication even when the problem is our own

• listen actively to our stakeholders and so hear the real message behind the words

• understand that problems that we perceive to be ours may in fact be the other person's

• enable and put into practice the problem-solving process for someone else.

9.Creating an Action List – Staff Inset Session

Introduction

Many ideas for practical action had been collected during the various stages of our work on vision and ethos up to this point. Initially we had intended to involve every stakeholder in contributing ideas for action and, to a large extend, this was achieved. As mentioned previously only one group of stakeholders had in fact been omitted (due to their working hours) but all others had been involved.

We therefore felt that we now had a useful set of ideas that could be acted upon. Before this could happen though it would be necessary to categorise this (very) long list under our four values headings.

Aims of the session

To examine and sort our list of actions into our four values headings:

1. Environment
2. Positive and productive relationships
3. Teaching and learning
4. Aesthetic and spiritual.

What we did

Time was precious and so to speed up the decision-making process I sorted as many of the actions as possible into the categories prior to the meeting. The organising process during the session was then a quick and painless exercise of checking what I had done and adding anything remaining in the list.

Using our interactive white board at this stage proved to be very useful as it allowed us to 'cut and paste' ideas easily. Alternatively, we could have worked on paper but this would have been less flexible and would probably have involved more 'tidying' of the data afterwards. I think this illustrates the need to consider any approach when visioning that will save time and effort.

The outcomes from this session are shown in the following sections.

Safe positive environment

We want Air Balloon Hill Junior School to be a safe, calm, welcoming environment where everyone takes pride in their surroundings.

To achieve this we will:

Play calm music in and out of the classroom.

Hall displays.

Fewer footballs and put away from main entrance.

Teach children how to play games in paired groups with teachers who know them.

Smaller football area.

Specific areas for games.

Create more stimulating environment.

Different zone in the playground.

Put up class displays.

Plants in class.

Reception should be first port of call – move reception.

Welcoming sign to school child design.

Clean new/update of toilets.

Air fresheners, towels and soap in toilets.

More signs to guide visitors especially reception.

Promotion of cleaner schools – picking up litter.

Plants and flowers.

Small removable work areas in hall.

Tidy cloakrooms with storage for PE kit

Reception area for parents/visitors.

Locking toilet doors.

More trees and benches.

Water fountains.

Drawers under desks.

New music room.

Murals on walls.

Clear signs to reception.

A welcoming sign.

Phone contact at gate to reception.

Road markings to reception.

Swap ICT suite with office.

Reconsider use of playground – football.

Ensure seating is suitable and resources are well maintained and appropriate.

Positive and productive relationships

We want Air Balloon Hill Junior School to be a happy community with respectful cooperative relationships.

To achieve this we will:

Focus only on the positive and keep rest for 1-1

Teach children how to play games in paired groups with teachers who know them

Promotion of good language

Encourage team spirit

Generate improved attitude to SMSAs and playground equipment

Time to talk about social issues

Find ways of engendering respect between pupils

Designated children to smile, greet and guide visitors to reception

Use of playground prefects

Buddy system to support Yr3

Movement of children outside heads's office at lunchtime, dining hall manners

Staff to greet visitors to classrooms

Reinforcement of greetings and thanks

Staff 'Good Effort' certificates

Doors to be held open

Interactive 'Manners' display to record positive actions

Circle Times on basic manners.

Teaching and learning

We want Air Balloon Hill Junior School to promote excitement in learning through supportive, stimulating teaching that is progressive and constantly evolving.

To achieve this we will:

Fewer worksheets

More fun activities

More flexibility

Discussion

Put up class displays

Allow time for children to produce quality work for display

Create more flexibility in the day to day management of the class

Encourage use of more collaborative and cooperative group work

Promote independent working

Use of praise when teaching

Varied approaches to teaching

More effective use of LSAs

Home/school links to support learning to be encouraged

Encourage pride in work by looking for good presentation.

Aesthetic and spiritual

> We want Air Balloon Hill Junior School to be an inspiring environment in which all individuals are cherished.

To achieve this we will:

> Wed /Thurs split up into lower and upper school service
> Calm music in and out of hall
> Children to participate in assemblies
> Class services – space/time for it to happen
> Create more stimulating environment
> Offer time for thought and contemplation
> To show appreciation for inspirational thoughts and ideas
> Encourage calm and inner stillness
> Help children to appreciate the beauty within the natural world.

Conclusion

We were now in possession of all the information needed for action. Our lists were complete yet still open for any new ideas. We all felt ready to make some fundamental changes to our school.

The key lessons learned from the session were as follows:

- During the initial stages of visioning everyone needs to be actively involved until consensus is reached.

- However, at later stages (where trust and understanding is established) a lot of effort can be saved if some preparatory work is carried out prior to each session, for example, sorting ideas for action ready for discussion.

- True and tried methods are the best but sometimes new technology can be used to good effect, for example, using the interactive white board with projector so everyone can be involved and changes easily made.

- Make use of appropriate categories to group and manage ideas better.

10. Prioritising and Allocating Responsibilities – Staff Inset Session

Introduction

This was the point where all our careful planning and preparation finally came together in readiness for us to take action.

It was decided that ideas for action should be considered separately under each of our values headings. We therefore used a series of four staff meetings to decide which targets we would address in each of the areas. This was felt to be an ideal number of sessions – enough to cover everything but not too many to cause a droop in our enthusiasm.

Aim of session

To prioritise actions and to identify people responsible for putting them into practice.

What we did

Initially we felt it important to identify targets that, in our opinion, would make the greatest difference to the school. It was felt important to select a manageable number of targets initially and leave some targets for the next round.

Four new tables were generated to record our targets that we called 'Values Statement Action Tables' (or VSATs for short). Each table had one of our values statements at the top to remind us of our purpose and consisted of three columns:

1. Desired outcomes.

2. Actions to be taken.

3. Person(s) responsible.

Copies of these can be found at the back of the book.

Although adding a cost column was also considered, we decided not to include one at this stage as we felt that finances for the vast majority of targets would be available to us.

In fact it was only in one instance that we encountered any 'problems' with money, and that was with the 'plants around the school' idea. The background and circumstances of this failure to act have been discussed previously but it would have been easy to achieve if the staff responsible had been given cash in hand to allow them to make immediate purchases. All other targets could be achieved without petty cash.

In other situations, however, I think it would be wise to include a cost column as it is likely to be an important consideration. If money is an issue then it will determine which actions can be taken now and which are deferred until funds are available.

As targets were selected and added to each 'Values Statement Action Table' it became apparent who would be best placed to take responsibility for them. Many actions needed to be steered by specific people such as the SMT or the caretaker, however there were some that naturally fell to other interested volunteers. It was not difficult to find these volunteers as in many cases the targets had stemmed from their ideas in the first place and so they were more than keen to see them through.

Initially we also attempted to categorise our targets into short, medium and long-term goals, (indicated by an 'S', 'M' and 'L' on the examples at the end of the book). It soon became clear though that we would have to abandon this idea as it was very difficult to account for the 'human element' when assessing timescales. You cannot assume that everyone else will be as enthusiastic as you or that they will work at a predictable or consistent rate.

For example

We thought that putting air fresheners and soap into toilets could be easily achieved. Unfortunately that was not the case, as the person responsible (the caretaker) had difficulty in remembering on a daily basis due to his own very heavy workload. This resulted in staff having to remind him when children made complaints that there was no soap in their toilets.

It was also interesting to see how new Government and LEA initiatives naturally slotted into one or other of our values areas. As the achievable targets tables grew it was exciting to see how our next School Improvement Plan could fit into these values. Everything seemed to be coming together at last and if everything we did within school fitted with our values then we knew that we were moving closer to our ultimate vision.

Conclusion

All was now in place and during the following day we set about achieving these targets. The head teacher put up copies of our targets in his office and was observed referring to them on a regular basis. He found this way of displaying our intentions very useful when meeting with inspectors and advisers.

The staff room also displayed these values tables as a daily reminder of our commitment and of progress made.

The Governors and children were also made aware of what we were attempting to achieve. Unfortunately, we realised that the parents had not been involved in this phase. The parents are powerful stakeholders that represent a veritable army of potential workers which can be used to support efforts such as this. By not involving them we had excluded a major source of help. We all agreed that this would need to be rectified at the review stage.

In order to maintain a sense of momentum we made a conscious decision to carry out regular progress reviews. A review period of less than two terms was therefore initially set.

The key lessons learned from the session were as follows:

- Ideas without action are not much use!
- Allocate responsibilities to those who have the interest and the enthusiasm.
- Consider all stakeholders as potential implementers (not just the staff).
- Implement those ideas with the biggest impact and lowest cost first.
- Be careful when estimating timescales – remember the human element.

11. Review of Progress – Staff Inset Session

Introduction

The review of our progress came around all too quickly. What had we achieved? During the weeks leading up to our first review there had appeared to be a significant number of changes made within the school environment. But how successful had we actually been? The purpose of this session was to find out!

Aims of session

- To take stock of achievements to date.
- To report on those targets achieved, those in-hand and those yet to start.

What we did

We needed to assess our progress quickly and efficiently as we only had one session assigned to this activity (the next session was allocated to setting new targets to move the school forward again).

Staff were split into four mixed-year groups for this session. Each group was given a different enlarged copy of our values table. Their task as a group was to discuss the targets and decide which of them we had completed successfully, which were still ongoing and which had not been started at all. This was indicated by annotations using pens and highlighters. Once completed, the values tables were then passed to a new group.

By the end of the session all groups had had the opportunity to discuss and annotate the sheets on the progress of all targets:

- achieved
- ongoing
- yet to be started.

These annotated sheets were then taken away by me, collated and analysed to establish the final consensus. The results of which can be found at the end of the book and a colour version printed from the CD-ROM.

The analysis took the form of colour coding, in a 'traffic light' report:

- Green – target achieved.
- Yellow – target ongoing.
- Red – yet to be started.

The VSATs now not only looked colourful but also felt much more immediate and informative. It was very satisfying to see such a lot of green and yellow. The red lettering however just seemed to leap from the page and these would need to be given priority consideration. Were we to continue with these or were they no longer relevant?

Another way of highlighting our progress was then to place the targets into three columns on a separate table – achieved, ongoing or not started. The achieved column certainly looked impressive and served as a motivator for us to take further action.

We felt that the results of our years work on vision and ethos needed to be advertised to all.

It was therefore decided to update our prospectus, website, school newsletter and letterheads to include our vision and values statements. In addition we wanted to celebrate our achievements in displays around the school, especially in the main hall for all to see and for us to refer to during school assemblies. This gave us all a sense of pride and shared ownership in the work we had done.

Conclusion

This session was very successful as it quickly showed how much we had achieved and what was yet to do. It also provided the ideal springboard for us to start thinking about the positive changes that had resulted from all this activity.

In particular I think the key lessons learned from the session were as follows:

- Be realistic with your estimate of progress – if nothing has happened be honest and say so.

- Take pride in your achievements and advertise them.

- Re-visit ideas that are not progressing and ask if they are still relevant.

- Make use of colour to give a clear indicator of progress.

- In order to get a balanced overview involve as many of the team as possible.

12. Assessment of Benefits – Staff Inset Session

Introduction

Projects such as this are largely concerned with change. Even if we were to achieve all the agreed actions, within the planned time and without exceeding the budget, we would not have really succeeded unless the desired change happens. Perhaps even more importantly this change must then lead to positive benefits for the school. It is therefore vitally important to try and quantify the changes that result from your new vision to see if the benefits have indeed been realised.

This is easier said than done however as change might have happened naturally anyway. Also, it is very tempting to see a positive change and put it down to something you have done when in fact it is nothing of the sort.

Bearing these cautionary words in mind I have attempted below to set out changes that we as a school feel have resulted from our work on vision and ethos. In order to make it easier to follow I have classified a selection of the more noticeable actions under the four main values categories we used earlier.

Safe positive environment

Reduce playground balls

Following on from our proposal to have fewer balls in the playground, and to use colour-coding to identify which year group the ball belonged to, it was pleasing to note how much calmer the playground felt. Children must now cooperate as a year group if they are to be allowed to use a ball and this has resulted in greater self-control. There has been a noticeable drop in the number of quarrels and arguments and fewer complaints to the support staff following disruptive incidents. There have been fewer complaints from parents and visitors who cross the playground during break-times and staff on playground duty feel a lot happier. This situation needs to be monitored regularly as 'boys will be boys' (and sometimes 'girls will be girls') resulting in an extra football sometimes surreptitiously appearing in the playground.

Litter

We now have a large number of new bins and have noticed a considerable decrease in the amount of litter around the school. Some of this effect has been due to another related initiative where children were encouraged to eat fruit rather than crisps and other unhealthy snacks. Even so we are not buried under a pile of orange peel or banana skins so we must assume the children are taking note and either taking the rubbish home or using the new bins.

Classroom organisation

As a result of our work several classrooms have now been refurbished and provided with new furniture. Using furniture of a modern design has allowed us to organise each classroom to suit the specific needs of that class. Instead of central storage we now have under-desk storage areas and this has led to a big reduction in movement and hence disruption within the classroom. The environment feels better organised and cleaner than before, things are easier to find and the children are more settled.

Positive and productive relationships

Appreciation of others

Staff are now putting theory into practice following on from our Inset sessions with Barbara and George. We are now all using positive, caring language with the children and words such as, 'Hello', 'Thank you,' and 'Sorry,' are being heard more frequently. This has led to a much calmer atmosphere throughout the school and generally less disruption.

Staff feel equipped to provide even better role-models for the pupils. These enhanced communication skills have plainly 'rubbed off' on the pupils resulting in increased trust and fewer problems. Again Barbara commented on this positive and calm feeling during one of her recent visits.

Questionnaires

As part of our ongoing quality control we have used questionnaires to assess the feelings of both children and parents across a broad range of school issues. The overall result from these exercises have been very positive. For example, the recorded instances of bullying in our school are very low, but perhaps more importantly, children feel they can talk to staff if they feel they are being bullied or unhappy in any way. Parents echoed this positive opinion and considered the school to be supportive.

This positive image has always been a hallmark of our school but I feel that our work on vision and ethos has helped to support this and possibly improve it further.

Teaching and learning

Health

As mentioned previously we now have much less litter around the school. This situation has been assisted by the healthy eating initiative which encourages children to consume more fruit and fewer snacks (such as crisps). Whilst the healthy eating regime is welcomed it has actually generated a new problem for us – smuggling! As can be imagined some children are still very fond of their crisps and snacks and will not give them up easily. We now have to be extra vigilant in spotting convenience food at a distance!

Independent learning

This is an ongoing project (supported by our work on vision and ethos) which aims to provide more flexible and imaginative lessons for 'pain free' learning. We encourage working with as many different mediums and media as possible (not just paper) in an effort to raise levels of enthusiasm and interest to new heights. For example, we recently undertook a lesson which used paint on paper but which was not a lesson in Art but RE! Initially the children were somewhat baffled as to why we were using paint in an RE lesson but all became clear once we had produced some very moving illustrations of the Crucifixion.

This sort of approach helps to unlock creativity and escape from the normal boundaries which limit exploration and learning. From my point of view it is very rewarding to see children become aware of their surroundings and themselves and start to get in touch with the inner person.

Aesthetic and spiritual

Lessons

This is an area that naturally dovetails into just about everything else. It is possible to explore inner thoughts and to discover feelings of a spiritual nature within the remits of the National Curriculum. It could be the feelings of rebirth and hope as the paintbrush touches the paper producing the dawn of the Resurrection in an RE lesson or perhaps the excitement and joy at discovering that there are infinite, and often amazing, patterns to be found when working with numbers.

Staff are increasingly trying a variety of ways to encourage the pupils to explore their thoughts and ideas in greater depth. The inset work to develop the Gifted and Talented pupils across the curriculum has been very beneficial to all in this respect. This work has hinged on the use of open questions which promote extensive answers and thoughts, often beyond the obvious. This has been deemed to be so important that work to promote the Gifted and Talented is included and highlighted on teachers weekly plans.

13. Looking Back (and Forward)

The first year of our work on vision and ethos has certainly born fruit and many practical improvements have been seen both in and around the school. It now has a different feel to that of a year ago with positive comments being received about how safe and calm it is. So it was with a sense of excitement and high expectation that we set about setting our new targets for the following year.

Our first task was to remove targets from our 'Values Statement Action Tables' that had been achieved. We also needed to revisit and rationalise ongoing or incomplete targets in a drive to create 'smarter' objectives. This made room for wishes that could not be included first time round and also freshly generated actions from our wide circle of stakeholders.

I think the important thing to remember about visioning is to keep up a sense of momentum and not to allow the process to drift or 'fizzle out'. This is a potential risk when new members of staff arrive and established members leave. How will you then ensure the new staff really do share and live the vision? If they don't of course then the whole process will be undermined.

In our school we have posted our targets on the staffroom wall for everyone to see. We encourage everyone to check these regularly as they are far from static. Although notice boards can be ignored this is less likely if the progress on your actions are on public display!

I would also consider covering the schools vision and ethos during staff induction and maybe providing them with an information pack outlining the key points. I would anticipate that new staff would take an interest in some of the ongoing actions and get involved in making them happen. We have set a review period for every year in the hope that, once they are committed to actions, staff won't forget about them and the momentum will be kept going.

As discussed previously, I feel that committing to action is the best way to generate enthusiasm and build a sense of 'ownership' in the visioning process. This is especially true if you have two people responsible for each action as they will tend to share the workload and possibly generate more 'offspring' ideas in the process. The danger to watch out for here is duplication of effort or the reverse – both people thinking the other is doing it!

What would we do differently next time?

Firstly I think I would set up a petty cash fund for actions that required immediate purchases. This was one area where we failed to implement at least one action – 'plants around the school'. With just a small cash fund (less than £100) we could easily have achieved this objective.

I think I would also ensure that we included all stakeholders from the outset. In our case we failed to engage stakeholders that worked non-office hours, for example, lunchtime and twilight staff, and this must be guarded against if you want a truly comprehensive vision. In order to reach these people next time I think we would utilise methods appropriate to them, for example, a questionnaire which they could complete in their own time rather than attempt to arrange a meeting in our own time.

We also failed to engage the parents at the implementation phase – a potentially vast reserve of untapped effort! In hindsight the question of 'how to get the parents doing' would have been a valid point for discussion at the early phases of the project. However, this is a potentially huge area for consideration and there is a danger of spending too much time on it.

The next step for us will be to add new and more adventurous targets to our wish lists and to find ways of including more of the stakeholders in implementing those goals. I am confident that this next important step will bring ever closer to our ultimate goal.

> We aim to provide an inspiring learning environment that values and develops everyone.

14. Ten Steps to Success

1. Involve the stakeholders

A stakeholder is defined as a specific person or group who has an interest (or stake) in the outcome of a project. They may be people who have to commit resources or funds to the venture or they may be directly, or indirectly, affected by the outcome.

In a school environment they include teaching staff, parents/carers, children, governors, LSAs, administration staff, caretaker, SMSAs and kitchen staff.

All these people can offer a worthwhile contribution to the project from a variety of perspectives. It is therefore very important that the views of all stakeholders are considered so that nothing is omitted. It is equally important that no-one feels overlooked as it's the stakeholders who can make or break the progress towards the end goal.

Don't forget that it can be very easy to overlook a stakeholder but very difficult to include them later!

2. Make a plan

It is very easy to get started with wild enthusiasm and soon have more ideas than you know what to do with but sooner or later these must be turned into a plan for action.

At the strategic level you will need to consider a number of questions. How will you turn that idea into reality? What resources will be needed? How long will it take? Who will be communicated with and how often? What information will be needed at each stage? How will we know we have succeeded?

The answers to these questions should then be formulated into an overall plan that is copied to everyone involved. At the more detailed level it is still important to set out a plan for key events.

For example, even during the initial phases, where new ideas are being generated, every meeting should have clear objectives and a fixed timescale to avoid unnecessary debate and ensure the relevant points are covered. Additional time may then be needed to collate ideas and organise the groups thoughts into some sort of logical form.

3. Assign responsibilities

During all phases it is important to assign responsibilities to people who are not only enthusiastic but who also possess the necessary skills. During the doing phase this is especially so. Nothing gets done without action and people need to know what is expected of them and by when!

When it come to turning our ideas into reality it is best to use volunteers as they are the ones who are motivated to succeed. These can come from within the school or from outside but wherever they come from it is important that they share your vision and implement the work quickly.

One pitfall to watch out for is letting one hyper-enthusiastic person do all the work! It is tempting to always use the most enthusiastic person but visioning is a shared process.

4. Communicate openly

How do we share our vision of the vision? This is a problem of communication, which in every organisation is one of the most difficult things to do properly, and the larger the organisation the greater the difficulty.

It is essential to determine who needs to know what and when, (including stakeholders). Governors, for example, who are ultimately responsible for the strategic control of the school, need regular updates on the schools progress towards all targets. In this way they will be able to proudly communicate to the outside world the ways in which their school is currently changing in order to raise standards.

Parents also need to be aware that their ideas have been used to promote change. Newsletters are the obvious choice here but the best way of communicating progress is to invite them on-site to see for themselves. Children also need to be made aware of what the vision is trying to do and their attention needs to be regularly drawn back to the underpinning values. School assemblies and posters could be used for this although every teacher who lives the dream will automatically be communicating it as they work.

Finally, a school's vision and values should be something to be proud of and promoted widely through media such as the website or prospectus.

5. Make it fun

We all learn more if we are having fun whilst doing it! Life becomes less of a drudge, we are allowed to be more creative and we share ideas. This is something of a luxury in the teaching profession but it allows us to work much more synergistically. Much of the work will need to be carried out after school and staff will naturally be tired. It is important therefore to keep it light and to set a manageable timeframe.

Vision and ethos is a serious subject but little progress will be made unless the sessions are light hearted and 'digestible'. To assist this process you should aim to always move from the known to the unknown and from the easy to the less easy. To help with removing mental 'blocks' all ideas should be treated as valid (even seemingly crazy ones) and everyone should have their say.

Small groups tend to work well during brainstorming sessions and the flow of good ideas can be lubricated with an informal approach. Regularly changing the groups around and ensuring a good mix of personalities and experiences will ensure a rich source of potential ideas.

Another powerful tool is 'counter planning'. The aim here is to generate as many ideas as possible that are the reverse of the intended outcome – in this case to make the school worse! These sessions are usually fun because people have free rein to come up with as many wild ideas as they like. Once this is done you should have a better picture of what you don't want your school to be.

6. Make it relevant

Work on vision should have a positive and measurable impact within the school. It is therefore vital that effort is directed toward tackling issues relevant to the needs of the school and not be seen as an opportunity to embark on a protracted discussion about what is wrong with the school!

There is also a very real danger that discussions relating to ethos become 'woolly' and vague and therefore difficult to implement in practice. During the early stages of the process a certain amount of creative thinking is needed but later on this needs to give way to more precise and relevant discussions.

7. Make it usable

As someone once said the only constant in life is change! Once we have formulated our vision and ethos framework it should be robust enough to withstand the inevitable changes that will occur within the school environment.

The core values of a vision and ethos framework should be universally applicable and so should never change but we need to accommodate new initiatives. These may be forced upon us from outside or maybe the result of internally driven change. Either way our framework should lend itself to different situations and needs and be in harmony with Government and LEA initiatives.

The wording needs to be 'user-friendly'. In other words it should be universally understood by using clear, non-ambiguous language, whilst avoiding esoteric statements, abbreviations, buzzwords and jargon. It should also be verifiable. In other words we should be able to show that what we have written is actually possible to do. Whilst this is somewhat difficult to achieve it should, nevertheless, be our goal.

8. Monitor progress closely

It is vital during the planning and doing phases that progress is monitored regularly against set targets. If this is not done then you will have no idea if you are on track and the whole process could suffer a lack of momentum. As with all projects the focus should always be on delivery.

Agreeing on realistic milestones and nominating someone who is responsible for achieving them is key to this process. We must also guard against 'drift' in the delivery dates or in the scope of what we are doing. It is very easy to put things 'on-hold' (during a period leading to an inspection, for example) or simply 'dumb-down' the outcomes (to save money, for example).

9. Ensure benefits are realised

Vision and ethos are a waste of time unless positive change happens as a result. This is the hardest part of the process to monitor and check but the one with the biggest payback. We could succeed totally in delivering what we said we would, but fail miserably in creating positive change as a result!

It is important to record at the outset what you intend to deliver at the end and what benefits you expect as a result. After the process is completed there is a temptation just to sit back and breath a sigh of relief whereas what we should be doing is checking that the vision is working.

The bottom line is to keep asking, 'Is all this effort making a difference?'

10. Live the vision

Having invested considerable time developing your framework, when it's done – do it! Your framework should be like a living and breathing entity, coursing through the veins of the school. Everyone should believe in it and practise its principles.

The framework will soon lose its practical value if the principles are not practised within the school. To help avoid this you could nominate a 'champion' to promote the principles of vision and ethos and who could challenge those who do not follow it. It is possible, of course, that there is a better way. If so we would need to know what it is and decide if it might be appropriate. Good luck!

Values Statement and Action Tables 1 – 8

Colour versions of the following tables are included on the CD-ROM.

1. Safe Positive Environment – Targets set

We want Air Balloon Hill Junior School to be a safe, calm, welcoming environment where everyone takes pride in their surroundings

Desired environment	Action/s to be taken	Person/s responsible
Air fresheners, towels and soap in toilets.	Air fresheners in all toilets. Paper towels, toilet paper and soap needs to be regularly checked and replaced (adults and children).	Caretaker.
Toilets to be updated.	One toilet block is being redeveloped already to include an accessible toilet. Others to follow in subsequent years.	Head teacher to overview.
Plants around the school.	Plants to be purchased for office/halls and playground/garden areas.	Teacher to buy them for school. Caretaker to water.
Welcoming sign with school logo.	Company to create the welcoming sign, including school logo.	Head teacher. Head teacher to discuss with Infant Head teacher.
Space in the playground and reduction in quarrels over balls.	Different colour balls for each year group. Trial of ball court at playtime.	Teachers on duty. Teacher to be in-charge of different colour balls.
Litter free playground.	Teachers to discuss collection of litter with children. New bins to be purchased. Mural to be painted in shelter.	All staff. Head teacher. Class council.
More colourful and stimulating playground.	Ask children about what they'd like painted on the ground in the front playground. Teachers to teach children how to play more games. Book to be ordered to get ideas/teachers to share ideas in planning and then to practise at a further point.	
Children to be taught new playground games and encouraged to play cooperatively.	On Fridays all staff to go out at break time (instead of a Circle Time) and play games with the children. Using the playground equipment.	Teachers in golden time/circle time. Teacher to order games book. Teacher to photocopy sheet of games and pass around.
Organisation of furniture in classrooms.	Volunteers LW/NC to research consortium and share ideas with staff – i.e. drawers under desk and ways to store PE kit.	Teacher to research.
Larger/extended music room.	Head teacher to research planning permission to extend music room and discuss possibility of using after school club.	Head teacher.

2. Safe Positive Environment – Review of Targets

We want Air Balloon Hill Junior School to be a safe, calm, welcoming environment where everyone takes pride in their surroundings

Desired environment	Action/s to be taken	State of Play – Completed? Ongoing? To be amended? Add comments where applicable.
Air fresheners, towels and soap in toilets.	Air fresheners in all toilets.	
Toilets to be updated.	Paper towels, toilet paper and soap needs to be regularly checked and replaced (adults and children).	Paper towels in classroom.
	One toilet block is being redeveloped already to include an accessible toilet. Others to follow in subsequent years.	
Plants around the school.	**Plants to be purchased for office/ halls and playground/garden areas.**	
Welcoming sign with school logo.	Company to create the welcoming sign, including school logo.	
Space in the playground and reduction in quarrels over balls.	Different colour balls for each year group.	Budget and time out of class needed.
	Trial of ball court at playtime.	Ball court at playtime.
Litter free playground.	Teachers to discuss collection of litter with children. New bins to be purchased.	Bin needed outside 5B.
More colourful and stimulating playground.	Mural to be painted in shelter.	
	Ask children about what they'd like painted on the ground in the front playground.	
Children to be taught new playground games and encouraged to play cooperatively.	Teachers to teach children how to play more games.	Need to teach games each year.
	Book to be ordered to get ideas/teachers to share ideas in planning and then to practise at a further point.	
	On Fridays all staff to go out at break time (instead of a Circle Time) and play games with the children. Using the playground equipment.	
Organisation of furniture in classrooms.	Volunteers LW/ NC to research consortium and share ideas with staff – i.e. drawers under desk and ways to store PE kit.	Several rooms refurbished. PE kit no longer in cloakrooms.
Larger/extended music room.	**Head teacher to research planning permission to extend music room and discuss possibility of using after school club.**	Too expensive, infants use after school. Needs more thought.

3. Positive and productive relationships – Targets set

We want Air Balloon Hill Junior School to be a happy community with respectful cooperative relationships

Desired Relationships	Action/s to be taken	Person/s responsible
Encouraging team spirit throughout the whole school.	To continue to use cooperative games in Circle Time and PE.	All staff.
	To make greater use of group work to promote cooperative learning.	
	To establish a routine of paired reading between Year 6 and Year 3.	Year 6 and Year 3.
	Encourage a greater awareness of team points, e.g. a visual display to show winning team.	Teacher.
	Teachers to become part of the school team system.	All staff.
	To insure new teachers feel included and informed as part of the staff team as swiftly as possible.	All staff, mentors, Year colleagues.
Welcoming visitors to the school.	Place emphasis on good manners throughout the school.	All children, all staff.
	Children to:	
	• smile, greet and guide visitors to reception and if required to take visitors round on a tour.	Teacher to look for manners poster in 'Incentive Plus' magazine.
	• open doors for adults to go through first	
	• keep play equipment away from doors.	Teacher to raise in Monday Service.
Promotion of good language in the playground.	Discussion with children on language that is/isn't acceptable at playtimes. Suggest alternative words!	
A positive school community.	Teachers to behave as positive role-models to set the standard for children to follow.	All staff.
	To engage in activities that promote positive feelings within every child, e.g. in Circle Time everyone should say something positive about a chosen child. Teacher scribes, laminates, child takes home.	
All staff to make sure they appreciate everyone.	Everyone to make time to say 'hello' or 'thank you' or 'sorry' to all members of staff and children, even during busy times.	All staff.
All children feel they have friendship circles and are part of their class.	All teachers to discover isolated children in their class, and make special efforts to involve them fully in class life, encouraging others to be their friends.	All teachers & SMSA's.

4. Positive and productive relationships – Review of Targets

We want Air Balloon Hill Junior School to be a happy community with respectful cooperative relationships

Desired relationships	Action/s to be taken	State of Play – Completed? Ongoing? To be amended? Add comments where applicable.
Encouraging team spirit throughout the whole school.	To continue to use cooperative games in Circle Time and PE.	Pack given to staff to teach games.
	To make greater use of group work to promote cooperative learning.	Research into new schemes of work
	To establish a routine of paired reading between Year 6 and Year 3.	
	Encourage a greater awareness of team points, e.g. a visual display to show winning team.	
	Teachers to become part of the school team system.	
Welcome visitors to the school.	To insure new teachers to feel included and informed as part of the staff team as swiftly as possible.	
	Place emphasis on good manners throughout the school.	
	Children to:	
	• smile, greet and guide visitors to reception and if required to take visitors round on a tour.	
	• open doors for adults to go through first	
Promotion of good language in the playground.	**• keep play equipment away from doors**	
	Discussion with children on language that is/isn't acceptable at playtimes. Suggest alternative words!	
A positive school community.	Teachers to behave as positive role-models to set the standard for children to follow.	
All staff to make sure they appreciate everyone.	To engage in activities that promote positive feelings within every child, e.g. in Circle Time everyone should say something positive about a chosen child. Teacher scribes, laminates, child takes home.	
	Everyone to make time to say 'hello' or 'thank you' or 'sorry' to all members of staff, and children even during busy times.	Highlighted by bullying questionnaire.
All children feel they have friendship circles and are part of their class.	All teachers to discover isolated children in their class, and make special efforts to involve them fully in class life, encouraging others to be their friends.	Buddies across year groups.
		Maybe link with paired reading.

5. Teaching and Learning – Targets Set

We want Air Balloon Hill Junior School to promote excitement in learning through supportive, stimulating teaching that is progressive and constantly evolving

Desired teaching & learning	Action/s to be taken	Person/s responsible
Promote independent learning.	• Training on creative learning in History. • Be flexible to modify work if the situation demands. • Consider variety of ways to record work. • Reduce low level demands. • Provide opportunities for children who finish early. • Train children to solve their own problems with opportunities to follow individual research projects that can be continued at home.	Teacher: All staff.
More effective use of LSAs.	• LSAs running specific programmes for SEN, not using them as differentiation. • EAL children highlighted and a specific LSA to work with them is being trained.	All staff.
Challenge appropriate to ability.	• High but achievable expectations of broad bands of ability. • Gifted and talented training is being carried out.	All staff. Teacher:
Begin to address issues in 'Every Child Matters'.	• SEAL initiative to be cascaded to all staff. • Healthy Schools Standards to be achieved.	Teacher:

6. Teaching and Learning – Review of Targets

We want Air Balloon Hill Junior School to promote excitement in learning through supportive, stimulating teaching which is progressive and constantly evolving

Desired teaching & learning	Action/s to be taken	State of Play – Completed? Ongoing? To be amended? Add comments where applicable.
Promote independent learning..	• Training on creative learning in History. • Be flexible to modify work if the situation demands. • Consider variety of ways to record work. • Reduce low level demands. • Provide opportunities for children who finish early. • Train children to solve their own problems with opportunities to follow individual research projects that can be continued at home.	Recommendations by HMI. Training by teacher in Gifted and Talented.
More effective use of LSAs.	• LSAs running specific programmes for SEN, not using them as differentiation. • EAL children highlighted and a specific LSA to work with them is being trained.	How effective are they? Assessment?
Challenge appropriate to ability.	• High but achievable expectations of broad bands of ability. • Gifted and talented training is being carried out.	
Begin to address issues in 'Every Child Matters'.	• SEAL initiative to be cascaded to all staff. • Healthy Schools Standards to be achieved.	Continue to examine in foundation subjects.

7. Aesthetic and Spiritual – Targets Set

We want Air Balloon Hill Junior School to be an inspiring environment in which all individuals are cherished

Desired aesthetic & spiritual	Action/s to be taken	Person/s responsible
Time for thought and contemplation.	Offer time for listening to music: • Cool down in PE and bubble music in music • Provide a moment silence for thinking time, either after a question or a pause for thought. • Use Circle Time for reflection on events during the week. • Give children an experience of empathising with others or characters.	All Staff
Children to appreciate beauty in the natural world.	Take opportunities to appreciate the world around us throughout the curriculum • Class visits to different locations. • Observation of seasons and how the world changes over time. • The weather, its ability to change our environment, behaviour our feelings and moods. • Natural phenomena can affect how and the way we live today.	
To encourage a more varied approach to School Assembly.	Offer the opportunity for a variety of people to lead services: • To invite guest speakers to services • Encourage children to share work and manage assemblies. • Any member of staff may choose to lead service. • To share work done within R.E. i.e. classes on a voluntary basis sharing the work they've done in class, in particular other world religions.	
Children to be able to think deeply and ask questions.	Allow opportunity for children to ask questions and share ideas without there having to be aright of wrong answer and appreciate each others ideas (reference G&T training).	

8. Aesthetic and Spiritual – Review of Targets

We want Air Balloon Hill Junior School to be an inspiring environment in which all individuals are cherished

Desired Aesthetic & Spiritual	Action/s to be taken	State of Play – Completed? Ongoing? To be amended? Add comments where applicable.
Time for thought and contemplation	Offer time for listening to music • Cool down in PE and bubble music in music. • Provide a moments silence for thinking time, either after a question or a pause for thought. • Use circle time for reflection on events during the week. • Give children an experience of empathising with others or characters.	Need to collate music for PE. And other times when appropriate. Other role-models – disabilities/ethnic.
Children to appreciate beauty in the natural world	Take opportunities to appreciate the world around us throughout the curriculum: • Class visits to different locations. • Observation of seasons and how the world changes over time. • The weather its ability to change our environment, behaviour our feelings and mood. • Natural phenomena can affect how and the way we live today.	Link the way we live to current events.
To encourage a more varied approach to School Assembly	**Offer the opportunity for a variety of people to lead services:** • **To invite guest speakers to services.** • **Encourage children to share work and manage assemblies.** • **Any member of staff may choose to lead service.** • **To share work done within R.E, i.e. classes on a voluntary basis sharing the work they've done in class, in particular other world religions.**	Needs developing – other faith speakers and business people to improve aspirations. Hall displays on theme. This is crucial.
Children to be able to think deeply and ask questions.	*Allow opportunity for children to ask questions and share ideas without there having to be a right of wrong answer and appreciate each others ideas (reference G&T training).*	

61

Summary – Targets covered in '05-06

Achieved	Ongoing	Yet to be started
Welcoming sign with school logo.	Air fresheners, towels and soap in toilets.	Plants around the school larger/extended music room.
Space in the playground and reduction in quarrels over balls.	Toilets to be updated.	To encourage a more varied approach to School Assembly.
Litter free playground.	Encouraging team spirit throughout the whole school.	
More colourful and stimulating playground.	Welcoming visitors to the school.	
Children to be taught new playground games and encouraged to play cooperatively.	Promotion of good language in the playground.	
Organisation of furniture in classrooms.	A positive school community.	
All staff to make sure they appreciate everyone.	All children feel they have friendship circles and are part of their class.	
More effective use of LSAs.	Promote independent learning.	
Challenge appropriate to ability.	Begin to address issues in 'Every Child Matters'.	
	Time for thought and contemplation.	
	Children to appreciate beauty in the natural world.	
	Children to be able to think deeply and ask questions.	